HEALING THE ORPHAN SPIRIT

LEIF HETLAND

Contents

Introduction

The orphan spirit is rampant in the church and in the world today and causing all kinds of chaos and destruction. There is an answer to this orphan spirit which is the spirit of adoption and the spirit of sonship. The Father is waiting for His sons and daughters to understand who they are and be the co-heirs He created them to be. The most perfect example of a son knowing his true identity, position, and inheritance was Jesus.

Jesus left His Heavenly home to be born on the Earth as a man, leaving His Father and even His godly nature behind. As a child, he was raised for a time in Egypt, having escaped Herod's mass execution in His earthly home. As he began his ministry, he was continually on the move with His disciples going from town to town and being unwelcome in many places. At this time he had no earthly home, yet he never felt the sting and pain of the orphan spirit because He was constantly with His Father.

Jesus said in John 3:13, "No one has ascended to heaven, but He who came down from heaven, that is, the Son of Man who is in heaven." Jesus, alone, of all men did not have the orphan spirit, for He never really left the Presence of the Father. He was at home wherever He happened to be physically because He and the Father never lost the connection…not until He took our sins and hung on the cross. There He partook of the orphan spirit when He cried out in anguish, "Father, why have You forsaken Me?" Only then did Jesus experience the pain of the orphan spirit, as He died to bring us back into that relationship with the Father.

Now we can come back home to the Eden the Father created for us and we can live from Heaven instead of toward Heaven.

CHAPTER ONE

THE ORPHAN SPIRIT

"For as many as are led by the Spirit of God, these are sons of God. For you did not receive the spirit of bondage again to fear, but you received the spirit of adoption by whom we cry out, "Abba, Father." The Spirit Himself bears witness with our spirit that we are children of God."

Romans 8:14-16 (NKJV)

Many of humanity's problems can be traced back to the orphan spirit. It is an ancient spirit unleashed upon mankind through the work of the Evil One. It is a spirit whose chief joy is to separate children from their Father. It is the same spirit that destroyed the relationship between God and Adam. It came from the heart of the serpent in the Garden of Eden, for he was and continually will be the first orphan. His primary goal is to turn everyone into a version of himself – fatherless, disinherited, and lost. Before he unleashed the orphan spirit into the world, the Garden of Eden was a perfect place to raise a family. The King of heaven desired to have a family which He could love for all eternity. He wanted to be a Father to His children and longed for their hearts to be knit to His.

ॐ ॐ

ADAM WAS THE SON OF GOD! ADAM WAS NOT JUST GOD'S MASTERPIECE; HE WAS GOD'S SON.

ॐ ॐ

It was the gospel writer Luke who pointed us in the right direction. Just like the apostle Matthew, Luke also traced the genealogy of Jesus and then presented the lineage of the Messiah. In the course of exploring the family tree of Jesus, Luke discovered something that would change the way we forever look at humanity and, ultimately, how we look at ourselves. This is what he uncovered through the help of the Holy Spirit: "...Adam, the son of God" (Lk. 3:38). Adam was the son of God! Adam was not just God's masterpiece; he was God's son. The LORD loved him and doted on him because he was a son.

Now we know the reason why Jesus kept calling the King of heaven "our Father." When the disciples asked Jesus to teach them how to pray, this is how Jesus demonstrated the model prayer. He said to pray like this: "Our Father in heaven..." Jesus could have used other titles such as LORD, Master, Majesty, Almighty, Jehovah or Creator, but he did not use those. Instead, He said, "Father." More than that, Jesus said that God is our Father.

THE FATHER'S EMBRACE

The Father's love brought Adam to life. With respect to the other created beings, God needed only to speak a word, and they came into being from nothing. However, in the case of Adam, the Father chose to come down, scoop some earthly mud, and begin to fashion Adam into His own image and likeness. The Father took special care in creating Adam; and, as a result, the first voice, the first face, the first touch and the first emotion that Adam experienced was that of a loving Father. So, from the very beginning, mankind was created for this kind of encounter: face-to-face with Father God.

જે જી

THE FIRST FACE, THE FIRST TOUCH AND THE FIRST EMOTION THAT
ADAM EXPERIENCED WAS THAT OF A LOVING FATHER.

જે જી

The same thing can be said of Eve. She was created in like manner; however, the material used was more sophisticated. It was not mud, but a single rib coming from Adam, and yet the same process was followed. God took special care in creating Eve. The Bible also says God brought the first woman to her husband. So, just like Adam, the first face she saw, the first voice that she heard, and the first emotion she felt was not of man but of her loving Father. She was also created to have a face-to-face encounter with Father God.

જે જી

THE FATHER'S GREAT LOVE AND EMBRACE WAS THE REAL CRADLE
OF CIVILIZATION.

જે જી

The Father's great love and embrace was the real cradle of civilization. It was in the hands of a loving Father that the first man and woman came forth.

This is a tremendous revelation! Regrettably, when we look around the world today, it is hard to believe the original spirit God gave to His children was a spirit of sonship and not the spirit of an orphan. Watching the six o'clock news gives us the opposite idea. Man's appetite for violence, greed, and corruption makes us want to think the world is full of orphans. It seems this planet is full of children without fathers – abandoned, abused, maltreated, and forgotten. On top of that, many children are being trained by man-made religions which are "fatherless" at the core. Orphan thinking is the reason there is a high crime rate and a psychosis that drives terrorists to blow up buildings and crash airplanes. It cannot be simply explained through the lack of parenting skills or the absence of biological fathers. It can only be understood through supernatural insight – that at the root of our problems is the orphan spirit.

THE FIRST ORPHAN

The orphan spirit is a foul spirit that was brought here by Satan, the destroyer, murderer and liar. The great irony of it all is that this same spirit was released to the world through one man, Adam, the son of God. (Lk. 3:37, Rom. 5:12). Let us go back to the Garden once again and see how the curse of the orphan spirit was brought down to earth.

Satan was there in the Garden watching through envious eyes. He was also absorbing everything through an insecure heart. It probably drove Satan mad that his former Lord and King wanted children. He, who was once the ultimate insider, had been booted out of heaven and was now an outsider looking in. The devil watched as the happy family took a stroll in the Garden of Eden. In the cool of the day they walked together – the Father, son, and daughter. Satan thought he should have been invited to this party; but, since he had not received a formal invitation, the only thing left to do was to crash the party and make everyone as bitter and disappointed as he was.

The Orphan Spirit sets itself against the Father's love

Before Lucifer became Satan, he was an archangel who had the same level of importance as Gabriel, the messenger, and as Michael, the warrior. He was formerly known as Lucifer, the Angel of Light. He must have been very beautiful and full of wisdom because light signifies not only visual delight but also symbolizes truth. Unfortunately, Lucifer thought he could be like God.

His splendor and great knowledge corrupted him and deluded him into thinking that he, and a third of heaven's angels, could defeat the forces of God. Simply put, pride came before the great fall. Lucifer said, "I will ascend to the great heights and wrest authority and dominion from the Almighty."

The following sections will help explain how Satan defiled himself in the Presence of God (Is. 14:13-14).

Self-Will. Lucifer said, "I will ascend to heaven." A self-centered mind-set was fully displayed here, and it is a spirit familiar to many of us. It is interesting to note that even children have this tendency – to do whatever they want to do, not considering whether it is, indeed, the will of their Father. They have no time to find out if their ambitions will bring real happiness or deep sorrow. The devil became the devil because he was headstrong and did not care what the Father had to say about his plans and activities.

For the devil, the most important thing is "self;" nothing else matters. Contrast this to the example of Jesus, who was always in the attitude of prayer. He spent time on his knees and did not make any major decision without first consulting the will of His Father. This is because Jesus had the heart of a Son, and it was always aligned with His Father in heaven. The orphan spirit, on the other hand, sets itself against the Father's love.

JESUS HAD THE HEART OF A SON, AND IT WAS ALWAYS ALIGNED WITH HIS FATHER IN HEAVEN.

~ ~

Self-Exaltation. Lucifer said, "I will exalt my throne above the stars of God." The devil wanted to be higher than God. This is in direct opposition to the spirit of Jesus, who loved nothing more than to come under submission to the will of the Father. Jesus was willing to submit even to the point of death. The devil, on the other hand, believed it was no longer necessary to follow God. To make sure his message was loud and clear, he decided to overthrow the Lord's kingdom. Therefore, instead of working in submission to the Father, the Father would be in submission to Lucifer.

Self-Enthronement. Lucifer said, "I will sit on the mount of the congregation." God wants to be Lord over our lives because He knows He is the only one who can do it righteously. But the orphan mind has a different value system and insists it can do a much better job. When the children of Adam – carrying the orphan spirit – were scattered all over the planet, they desired to build their own kingdoms and their own systems of governance, without considering if they were in alignment with their Father in heaven. When Jesus came to earth, the devil brought Him to a high peak and showed Him the kingdoms of the world and their splendor. Satan said he would give all of those kingdoms to Jesus on the condition that the Son of God would bow down and worship him. However, Jesus, knowing what the serpent was up to, said: "Away from me, Satan! For it is written: 'Worship the Lord your God, and serve him only' "

(Mt. 4:10, NIV).

Self-Deification. Finally, Lucifer said, "I will be like the Most High." This is the highest form of self-glorification. This is the attitude that fuels Satan's rebellion against the Almighty. Again, this is in direct contrast to the attitude of the Son of the living God. The Father was pleased with His Son because, although Jesus possessed power and glory, He was willing to be under His Father's authority. The following is an expression of the Father's heart towards His Son and our attitude should be the same as that of Christ:

Who, being in very nature God, did not consider equality with
God something to be grasped, but made himself nothing, tak-
ing the very nature of a servant, being made in human likeness.
And being found in appearance as a man, he humbled himself
and became obedient to death – even death on a cross!

(Ph. 2:5-8, NIV)

Satan said, "I Will," instead of saying, "Thy Will be Done."
(Isaiah 14:13-14)

Satan did not have the same mindset Jesus had. Satan wanted to be equal with God and resented the idea of serving the King; therefore, instead of being obedient, he decided to start an uprising. Unfortunately for Lucifer, he was dead wrong. When Lord's former chief minister, worship leader, and anointed cherub, who walked among the fiery stones in the sacred realms of God, fell from heaven, it was a great fall. (Ez. 28:14).

When the dust of war settled, a terrible sight was revealed. There, in the center of the battlefield, stood a dark, brooding army. Their leader was defiant even in defeat. From that day forward, Lucifer was given a new name and would be known as Satan, the destroyer, accuser, and slanderer. He was also kicked out of heaven, for he had made his spirit so repugnant he could never be reconciled to his Maker. He would become the dragon, who swore enmity against God and against everything that He loves. Before Satan fell like lightning from heaven, he came face-to-face with the LORD, and he made a chilling promise that he would devote his remaining time on earth to steal, kill, and destroy.

His heart was filled with all kinds of wickedness and all his thoughts were evil; he was the ultimate adversary to a God who is full of goodness, kindness, mercy, and truth. Furthermore, when Satan decided to live outside God's realm and believed that he could thrive independently of God's love and sustenance, he became an orphan. By doing so, he also released the orphan spirit to the whole world.

We have been taught that God loves us. We also know that Jesus cares for us. Somehow, the way we understood it was that if we had a problem, we could go to Jesus, and Jesus would go to Daddy God and talk to Him about it. Jesus would make it okay. We also knew that when we came to the cross, we received forgiveness for our sins. We received healing. We received deliverance. But we have never realized the ultimate goal of Christ was to take us from the cross to our home with the Father. Our mind could never see it that way because we had no idea that before the Fall of Man, we were all part of God's family. We are God's children.

AWAY FROM HOME

God opened the eyes of Luke and brought him to the Book of Beginnings where he saw Adam walking with God as a son. When God created Eve, we were given undeniable proof that, in the very beginning, the Father wanted family – sons and daughters who would eventually give birth to future generations of godly human beings made in the image of God. They would be like their Father in heaven and rule their respective domains. (Gen. 1:28). He also gave them a home.

~ ~

WE HAVE A FATHER IN HEAVEN WHOSE CHIEF JOY IS TO GIVE US
LOVE, PEACE, JOY, SECURITY, AND ABUNDANCE.

~ ~

We have a Father in heaven whose chief joy is to give us love, peace, joy, security, and abundance. We can only find these things in a home. Therefore, the Garden of Eden was the first home created for man and woman. It was the most special place ever created, a place where heaven intersects with earth. The garden was the home that He had created for His first son and daughter. It was a perfect place where there was love, peace, and abundance. Food was everywhere, and no one had to labor in order to eat. It was a blessed place, a mini-version of heaven. Yet, the only reason it was a home was because there was a connection between the Father and His children. Without the Father's love, the Garden of Eden would have been just an ordinary place.

~ ~

HOME IS WHERE THE PRESENCE OF THE FATHER IS.

~ ~

Home is where the presence of the Father is; and, as long as Adam and Eve stayed connected, everything would have been perfect. But something terrible happened; the devil came in to disrupt the bond between Father, son, and daughter. The devil, the first liberal theologian said, "Did God really say…?" (Gen.3:1, NIV). Adam and Eve doubted the goodness of God and disobeyed His command not to eat from the tree of the knowledge of good and evil. Afterwards, they felt fear and shame; and, finally, they had to leave their home in the same way that Lucifer had to leave his original home in heaven.

We can see here that the orphan spirit was released and activated after the loss of a home. A home is not a physical structure but a place where there is the assurance of unconditional love. Thus, in a real home, there is warmth, security, provision, guidance, joy, peace, and abundant life. The person with an orphan spirit does not have access to these things. He lives life as if he has nowhere to go, as if he has no home.

The Orphan Spirit is released
and activated after the loss of a home.

It must also be made clear that the connection to the Father can be cut-off when we sin and when sin is committed against us. When I was twelve years old, an abuse took place in my life. I could not talk to anybody about it, so I started to hide and to cover it up. Does this sound familiar? Adam and Eve hastily assembled a covering made of fig leaves because they were ashamed of their nakedness. I, too, felt ashamed and very insecure. This started my path to living the orphan life-style, doing things on my own and existing as if there was no one there for me. The next five years of my life were spent in rebellion against my parents, the school, and other authority figures.

Those years were spent in the "pig pen" as I struggled to be free from addictions and other things. My parents sent me to a boarding school in Gjovik, Norway, but it did not take long before I was kicked out from that school. During that time, my name was in two national newspapers explaining that I had been forced to leave school because of drug abuse. There also followed a time when I lived in a park in Oslo, Norway – just like the prodigal son in the Bible story. After that I decided to come home. When I came in through the door of my parent's house, I was surprised to find that my fifteen-year-old brother had prepared for me a big cake which said: "Welcome Home, Leif." Not only did I come home to my family and my parents, but it was also during this time I came home to Father God as well.

The orphan spirit cannot be cast out. It cannot be forced out of our systems. It can only be healed. Healing can only be found in the Father's house. We need to learn to find our way home. The Father is waiting there for us. Let us come home to Him and experience His love.

REFLECTION

Take time to reflect on what the original atmosphere of our home was like in the Garden, a place of perfect peace, security, beauty, creativity and love.

ACTIVATION

1. Father, are there any areas in my life where I live outside that perfect place of peace, security, beauty, creativity and love?
2. Father, are there any areas in my life where I reject or am uncomfortable with your love?

DECLARATION

Father, from the very beginning your plan was for me to be your son/daughter. You are my place of perfect peace and love. I am completely safe and secure in your presence. Your presence is where I find and know who I am. I will rest in your arms my loving Father.

CHAPTER TWO

LIFE WITHOUT A HOME

Home is the place in all this world where hearts are sure of each other. It is the place of confidence. It is the place where we tear off that mask of guarded and suspicious coldness which the world forces us to wear in self-defense, and where we pour out the unreserved communications of full and confiding hearts. It is the spot where expressions of tenderness gush out without any sensation of awkwardness and without any dread of ridicule. – Frederick W. Robertson

Jack Frost was one of the first to clearly articulate the meaning of the orphan spirit and why the world needs to know and the Body of Christ needs to understand its implications. In his book, From Slavery to Sonship, he says that a person with an orphan spirit lives life as if he does not have a home. How terrible it is for someone to go through life without a home. A home can mean so many things to us. It is a place of both refuge and nurture. It is where we go after a very tiring day. It is a place of comfort when the world knocks us down. It is an oasis where worn-out spirits are healed and rejuvenated. It is a place of learning where we are taught how to deal with life's challenges. This is why we have to ask: How can a person live life without a home?

A true orphan knows what it means to live life without the security, stability, and warmth of a physical home. A spiritual orphan is not any different. He is also well-acquainted with the feelings of fear, rejection, anxiety, and homelessness even if he has a place to go home to at night. This is because the spiritual orphan has come face to face with the real meaning of homelessness – living life without a father. The inability to connect with a father can bring a son to a place of desolation. In the spiritual realm, he is like a wanderer in a barren region, unable to find peace, satisfaction, and purpose in life.

It is interesting to note that the Bible is full of commands and words of encouragement concerning widows and orphans. In ancient societies these social tags reduced a person to nothing. Thus, the Lord wanted everyone to pitch in and help those unfortunate enough to be labeled as widows and orphans. However, the thing we need to focus on here is this: a child is automatically an orphan the moment his father is no longer there to provide, protect, and care for him. Even if the mother is still alive, the child has now become an orphan. The ancient world realized there is something about a father's love and embrace that is vital; consequently, in a home without a father, his absence is seen as a deathblow to the family. Even in progressive societies where single mothers and widows have the ability to earn a living without their husbands, the absence of the father still creates a terrible void within the family. Without the presence of a father, there is an inner turbulence which greatly affects the children. This is what we mean by having an orphan spirit. It is when the children have the feeling of life without a home because they no longer have the benefits of a good and gracious father.

AWAY FROM HOME

The orphan spirit was released to the world by the first man and woman. They disobeyed a very important command which was not to eat from a particular tree. The tree of knowledge bears a special fruit that will make one wise in his own eyes, allowing that person to know good and evil. This new "wisdom" gave Adam and Eve the ability to think independently of God's counsel, a skill that quickly became a liability and a burden that the Father does not want His children to carry. The moment Adam and Eve chose to eat the forbidden fruit, they consequently chose to chart their destiny without the help of anybody. This new-found freedom had a terrible price tag. They had to learn to live on their own outside the Garden of Eden, their God-given home.

In the very beginning, they had lived a life of dependence and intimacy with Father God. However, after they ate the fruit, they immediately made the first independent decision outside the will of the Father. After that, there was no turning back. The orphan mindset established a precedent of disobedience and independence which became habit-forming behavior influencing all their further decisions. Moreover, it was more than just a habit: it was the very nature of the First Orphan, Satan, which they inherited through deception, and which, in turn, corrupted their being. Hence, the fallen nature took over the heart of mankind from then on. It created a pattern of living that brought about sickness, destruction, pain, and hardships in their lives and throughout the Earth.

The first ill-advised thing Adam and Eve did was to fashion clothes from fig leaves; however, it was not enough to cover them.

This was the first instance where human beings tried to solve problems on their own; but it proved to be a disaster rather than a cure. Instead of providing a solution, it led to greater and greater heartache for they now felt they could find a solution to their own problems without hearing the voice of the Father. They could "cover" their sin and disobedience by making themselves look right in their own eyes and by justifying their own actions.

The second thing they did was to hide from the presence of God. It was a willful choice. The Father did not want them to hide from His Presence, and yet they did. Fear and shame were the automatic penalty for sin. They tried to hide and cover themselves; yet, they could not get rid of their fear and shame. They tried to "fix" themselves, but everything they did was futile. Their self-will created the reverse effect: it drove them deeper and deeper into sin because their shame and guilt separated them from the Father's love. Consequently, they no longer turned to Him for guidance. Instead, they trusted their own wisdom which was now corrupted.

In their desperation, the third thing they did was blame others for their failures. The husband blamed the wife, and the wife blamed the intruder. Neither took the first step of ownership to confess the sin. Instead, each one was trying to hide from God's gaze, not realizing it is only in the Father's presence where everything can be restored to its original state.

They learned to speak lies, to cover-up, to hide, and to slander each other; and this began a process which would lead them to the path where "self" is the center. In the background, Satan was laughing and rejoicing because he had succeeded in transferring his "orphan spirit" into the hearts of God's children.

Finally, Adam and Eve had to leave the Garden of Eden because they might discover the Tree of Life and eat its fruit. We can only imagine what the consequences of that discovery could have been. They were already acquainted with the ways of evil and were handicapped with the orphan spirit. If they had suddenly become immortal after consuming the fruit from the Tree of Life, imagine the destruction they could have been capable of doing to each other, to their offspring, and to God's creation. (Gen. 3:22). Thus, Adam and Eve had to leave home; and so began mankind's struggle for survival without a Father to guide, to nurture, and to protect them.

FEAR AND SHAME

Adam and Eve were not born orphans, but they acquired the orphan spirit the moment they left the Presence of God and lived outside His domain. From that day forward, they had to deal with the outside world on their own. As a result, they made poor choices and one catastrophic decision after the other. They used to live life in total freedom and without worries, but after they left their home, they felt the full impact of fear and shame. This mentality and the emotions that come along with it were passed on from one generation to the next.

Once again, the Book of Beginnings, Genesis, is an indispensable tool that will help us understand what really happened to mankind after Adam and Eve ate the forbidden fruit. The Bible provides more than enough details regarding the tragic outcome of that event:

Then the man and his wife heard the sound of the LORD God

LIFE WITHOUT A HOME

as he was walking in the garden, in the cool of the day, and they hid from the LORD God among the trees of the garden. But the LORD God called to the man, "Where are you?" He answered, "I heard you in the garden, and I was afraid because I was naked; so I hid" (Gen. 3:8-10, NIV)

We can see here the dual outcome of sin: fear and shame. It does not matter if we are the perpetrator or if we are the victim. The same thing can happen to us all. Sin produces fear and shame in the life of man and woman. Fear and shame is released and activated not only in the heart of the person who sinned but also in the heart of the injured party who is the recipient of sin. The effect of sin is shared by both perpetrator and victim. For example, the victim gets violated and feels shame. The victim sometimes cannot talk about the offense because, at times, he thinks he is at fault, and then he is terrified of the prospect of being found out. There is a feeling of nakedness which will make that person feel of little value.

Furthermore, the offense also presents penalties for the offender. The perpetrator realizes there is a consequence every time he breaks the laws of God. When the offender feels ashamed of what he has done, he then becomes afraid; therefore, he hides from the authorities because he knows he has done something wrong. Adam and Eve felt the double impact of such fear and shame.

The person with an orphan spirit has to constantly deal with fear and shame, just as Adam and Eve did. However, modern man has mastered the art of hiding his true feelings from God and his fellow man. We know it is not good to be afraid. The world constantly reminds us that only weaklings feel fear. This idea has become so systemic that we have developed the ability to hide it from others. In movies, books, TV, and in the communities where we live and work, the concept of fear has become taboo. The fearful are labeled pathetic, and so we learn to mask that fear and hide it from the world and each other. We learn how to replace it with something else. Thus, the person struggling with fear will never acknowledge this struggle in public. He learns to release his fears when he is alone, where no one can see the agony within.

Man deals with fear by pushing it deep down in his spirit; and, since he does not allow the Father to remove that fear, he begins to struggle and try to handle it on his own. Instead of acknowledging fear within our inner-core, we learn how to be self-reliant, thinking we can fight off the rising dread within our spirit. The moment we begin to succeed a little, this self-reliant attitude gets escalated to pride. After that step, pride gives birth to arrogance.

If we fail, which we are prone to do when we work outside the will of God, we cope with fear through the outbursts of anger; or we do the opposite and turn the emotion inward and retreat within ourselves. We use anger to hide our fears and to assert control because we believe the world will unravel if we do not do something. We are constantly pressured to fix everything on our own. We retreat because we are afraid to deal with the real situation at hand for it might hurt too much. We think if we ignore the problem or dilemma, it will just go away.

We turn our hearts to steel, thinking that, if we make our inner-being as tough as a rock, we might become impervious to the sting of failure and rejection. In order to sustain that tough exterior, we learn how to reject the love, comfort, and admonition we receive from other people. We live life without a home while we try to create the self into an island fortress, striving to be self-sufficient and having the ability to go through life without experiencing the rewards of fellowship and true friendship.

A deep-seated fear drives us to succeed at all costs. We are even willing to cut corners in order to appear successful. Instead, deep down we know the truth; so we feel ashamed of ourselves. Shame is also a topic that the world does not want to discuss. The result is that, instead of asking for help, the orphan spirit in us forces us to hide this negative feeling from others; therefore, we learn how to pretend everything is perfect. However, the more we pretend, the more insecure we become. We try our best to overcome this awful feeling but realize we do not have the power to defeat it.

When the feeling of shame and hypocrisy overwhelms us, we begin to indulge in escapism. Alcohol, drugs, and pornography become the favorite of many. But our escapisms can also be more socially acceptable like losing oneself in relationships, drowning oneself in books, video games, television, the computer, or being a workaholic. In these instances, we can sometimes justify our escape patterns because the things we are escaping to are not "sins." Nonetheless, addiction sets in; and, before we know it, we are already neck-deep in the devil's quicksand. Instead of crying out for help and asking Father to come and rescue us, we try to crawl and claw our way out, only to find ourselves sinking even deeper.

REBELLION AND RELIGION: COPING WITH FEAR AND SHAME

All of us were created to live in the presence of the Father. Man can only be satisfied if he finds his way back to the Father and say with all confidence: "He who dwells in the shelter of the Most High will rest in the shadow of the Almighty." (Ps. 91:1). Our Father wishes us to reside in His presence; yet, since we are no longer familiar with His voice, His touch, and His emotions, we have to relearn everything that was lost in the Garden of Eden.

&~ ~&
ALL OF US WERE CREATED TO LIVE IN THE PRESENCE OF THE FATHER
&~ ~&

The first thing we need to learn is how to differentiate between the fear of the Lord and the fear of God's presence. The fear of the Lord is the beginning of wisdom. (Pr. 9:10). We are commanded to be in awe of God so we can understand the superiority of His ways and obey Him. However, we were never told to fear the presence of God. This is very clear even in the Old Testament when God spoke to His prophet and said, "Come now, let us reason together." (Is. 1:18, NIV). We also read David's tender words declaring, "The LORD is my shepherd..." It is difficult to imagine David fearing God's presence. Yet, if we do not understand the ways of the Father, then it is perfectly understandable why we are afraid when God is near.

&~ ~&
IF WE DO NOT UNDERSTAND THE WAYS OF FATHER, THEN IT IS
PERFECTLY UNDERSTANDABLE WHY WE ARE AFRAID WHEN GOD
IS NEAR
&~ ~&

Fear creeps into our hearts because, in reality, we do not trust God. This is another manifestation of the orphan spirit—the lack of basic trust. We see evidence of man's distrust against God through the internet; we can hear it in the media; we feel it in our schools and offices. People are unable to trust God. We are not sure if He will deal with us kindly, so, we are utterly terrified with the idea of drawing near to develop an intimate relationship with Him.

Since we feel we can no longer trust God, our interpretation of His Word is tainted with this unhealthy fear of His presence. Instead of seeing the commandments as coming from the heart of a loving God, we see them as restrictions. The laws of God are seen by many as a test instead of as signposts which would lead to a blessed life. Thus, there are two ways the orphan spirit will cope with this fear of Father. The orphan spirit will either rise up in rebellion or establish a religion.

THE ORPHAN SPIRIT WILL EITHER RISE UP IN REBELLION
OR ESTABLISH A RELIGION.

We can see the link between rebellion and the lack of trust in the book of Exodus when the newly freed Hebrew slaves were more than willing to go back into bondage simply because they could not believe the Lord would fulfill His promise to bring them to a land flowing with milk and honey. One glance at their immediate circumstances forced them to conclude that God had brought them into the desert to die. Their lack of basic trust did not allow them to see they were merely passing through the desert; it was not their final destination.

Another way to deal with our fear of Father's presence is to create a religion around God. This way the individual can control the Lord. In the mind of the spiritual orphan, Father is someone who is bad or who cannot be trusted. Consequently, in order to avoid close contact with God, man creates his own religious laws and practices to deceive himself and others. He assumes that formalities and adherence to a man-made code of beliefs will justify his lack of true contact with the Father.

Nevertheless, the spiritual orphan is quick to realize that we need God's provision and protection. We need abundant harvests. We need protection from our enemies. We need a vibrant economy. We need all these things; but since we are not willing to enter into an intimate relationship with Father, we try to keep God in a box. Sometimes the box is small like the religious object we hang around our neck, or it is as big as a multi-million dollar church complex designed to present our own version God, a deity who does not talk to or does not know how to relate to His own people.

We deal with shame in the same way–through rebellion or religion. The result of sin is shame which covers us like sores cover a leper. We want to get rid of the shame, but we feel naked in the eyes of God and man. We are desperate for favor, but instead we receive ridicule.

Many choose to rebel instead of putting up with shame. They flaunt their sinfulness for the whole world to see. They go out into the streets at night to influence others to follow in their footsteps. They have given up hope that God will ever forgive them.

The religious person, on the other hand, tries to deal with shame by attempting to appease God with good deeds and ritualistic sacrifices. We try to clean up our act, and yet we still feel rotten to the core. The person with the orphan mindset can be as religious as the Pharisees, yet never finds peace. This is because fear can only be displaced by Father's perfect love and shame can only be covered with the righteousness of Christ.

༄ ঔ

FEAR CAN ONLY BE DISPLACED BY FATHER'S PERFECT LOVE AND SHAME CAN ONLY BE COVERED WITH THE RIGHTEOUSNESS OF CHRIST.

༄ ঔ

CASTING OUT FEAR AND SHAME

We keep on striving and we keep on fighting. We think we have only two choices: rebellion or religion? We think we are confined to only two options. However, Jesus came to show us that there is another way. Father God is so in love with mankind that He gave His only begotten Son to show us the right way and to die in our place. The Father is more than willing to bring us back to our rightful place, to live in His Presence. He has proven His commitment by bringing His only Son to the altar of sacrifice. He told Abraham to hold back the dagger, but Father did not withhold His Son. He allowed the world to defile and crucify His precious Son. Even though His Son cried out, "Why have you forsaken me?" Father refused to answer because He knew it was the only way we could be restored to Him. Father God is waiting outside His home, and He is on the lookout for his prodigal and religious sons. He is waiting for both the prodigal and religious children who continue to strive far away from His

Presence. The table is set and the entire house has been prepared for your homecoming. The only thing missing is you. Start the long journey home. Father is waiting for you.

REFLECTION

Invite the presence of the Father and ask Him to go deep into your spirit and just let Him love on you for a while.

ACTIVATION

1. Father, show me if there is any way in which I live or behave as if I have no home.
2. Father, are there any areas in my life where I protect myself from rejection?
3. There is no fear in love and perfect love casts out fear. So, Father, show me any place in my life where fear is stronger than love.

DECLARATION

Father, I know you did not give me a spirit of fear or shame! You fashioned me from your likeness and made me YOUR son! You are my Father! I know you have plans to prosper me and not to harm me, to give me a hope and a future. I trust you completely! Remove my fears and replace them with your perfect love!

CHAPTER THREE

REBELLION OR RELIGION

"And I will pray the Father, and He will give you another Helper, that He may abide with you forever – the Spirit of truth, whom the world cannot receive, because it neither sees Him nor knows Him; but you know Him, for He dwells with you and will be in you. I will not leave you as orphans; I will come to you."
John 14:16-18 (NKJV)

It is easy for us to spot the bad guy in the story. We can see it in his actions and his words. We cannot say the same thing when it comes to the good guy, especially in movies and novels where there is a twist at the end. Those whom we thought are good are actually corrupt at the very core. Sometimes they hide behind a cloak of respectability. They are masters of the etiquette game and know how to impress the crowd, their peers, and especially their families. This is what we will discover in the parable Jesus preached to the crowd. As we study the Parable of the Lost Son, all eyes are expected to be focused on the prodigal son. Yet, in reality, there are two sons in the story—the prodigal son and the religious brother. They represent all of God's lost children on earth. The first one thought he did not need his father, and the other one thought he did not have a father.

Jesus taught this parable early in His ministry. It was so popular that Luke included it in his collection of short stories. The parable was like a tightly-coiled ball full of energy and passion having never a dull moment. Even at the very beginning, the audience was already captivated when Jesus described the audacity and callousness of the younger son demanding his share of the father's estate; and yet, when Jesus finished telling the story, the audience was left scratching their heads because there were two sons who both lived outside their father's love. The first one was rebellious and the other one was devout, but neither of them could understand their father's heart.

THE REBELLIOUS SON

We do not need to be told how inheritance is passed on from generation to generation. We know that, in most cultures, inheritance is given from father to son. It is also common knowledge that the son has to wait, in most cases, for the last will and testament prepared by the father. In other words, we are to wait for the Father's will. However, the younger, prodigal son could not wait. He did not want to go through the process of sonship; and, therefore, he demanded his share of the inheritance even though his father was not yet ready and willing to give it to him. By the son's actions, he was actually saying he wished for the death of his own father. There is an eerie similarity to Satan's desire to steal heaven from Father God and dominate it for his own pleasure.

The younger son personified the orphan spirit, which is a willful disposition that sets itself against the Father's love. The younger son said, in effect, "Give me what is mine because I want to live outside your will." He said his own will must be done, and the father had no right to tell him what to do. Amazingly, the father was so gracious he was willing to lose his property even though he knew very well his irresponsible son would just squander away his inheritance. So, the father divided the property between the two sons. Then the younger one sold his share to accumulate liquid assets. After a few days, he started his journey into a distant country, creating as much distance as he could away from his father.

We have to understand that this is more than an issue of money. The younger son wanted to have total control over his own life and did not want the guidance and approval of his father. We, like Adam and Eve and the prodigal, flee the presence of the Father when we find ourselves in rebellion and willfulness.

The Orphan Spirit will lead us away from home.

With his pockets overflowing with inheritance money the younger son decided it was time to forget all the things his father had taught him. He decided it would be best to let "self" be the king over his life. From that day forward, he would not be guided by the law of love but by his sensual desires.

Jesus said the prodigal consumed everything he had through wild living (Lk. 15:13). He did not invest wisely, and so it did not take long for everything to disappear. His so-called friends also left him, and he later found himself alone and destitute in a foreign country. Then his world was turned upside down. A severe famine struck the land where he was living, turning a personal problem into a tragedy. He could not get a decent job because the whole nation was reeling from the impact of famine; everyone was almost as poor as he. He was forced to hire himself out to a pig farmer. But, make no mistake, this is not a sophisticated animal farm, and the prodigal son was never treated like a human being. In fact, he was treated a little lower than slaves, as the pigs were considered more important than he!

There was a time he became so hungry he begged to eat pig food. We know he begged his master to give him a portion of the animal feed because Jesus said his handlers refused to give him any (Lk. 15:16).

Look at the prodigal son—dirty, tired, and weak from lack of food and living in an environment to which he was not accustomed, and you can see a powerful image of the consequence of rebellion – the insistence that we can live outside the Father's embrace.

At home, the younger son had thought he was missing out on life and felt he did not have the freedom to do the things he really wanted to do. He had blamed his father for being strict like a tyrant having absolute control over him. However, in the pig pen he realized the real tyrant was the "self." His self-will drove him to the pits of despair and into a spiritual pigsty. He also then began to compare his current status to the servants who worked for his father, and he concluded that they were better off than he. The prodigal son said, "How many of my father's hired men have food to spare, and here I am starving to death!" (Lk. 15:17, NIV). Then it hit him like a thunderbolt–his father was a good father.

Sometimes we have to ask ourselves if we really know that we have a good Father. Being the by-product of a dysfunctional family may make it difficult for some people to understand the concept of both "good" and "father" in relation to each other. For many, it seems to be a misnomer to place these two terms side-by-side. The emotional trauma caused by betrayal, abandonment, and infidelity blinds us from the reality of a wonderful Lord and Savior seeking and calling those who have gone astray.

Others have taken for granted the goodness of the Father. Jesus said, "He causes His sun to rise on the evil and the good, and sends rain on the righteous and the unrighteous." (Matthew 5:45). The kindness of God surrounds us. It is this unconditional love and the repetitive nature of His blessings that sometimes dulls our senses.

The prodigal son went through life without taking time to reflect or to be grateful that he had a loving father. The younger son found himself in a place where he was able to recognize the difference between the world and the father's home, and the Bible says, "he suddenly came to his senses" (Lk. 15:17). He knew in an instant there was nothing else he could do except to seek his father's face and beg for mercy. Only one thing had been stopping him: his belief that no one could accept a rebel such as himself.

The people listening to Jesus telling the story could relate to the younger son's dilemma. In ancient societies the honor of the father and the honor of the family were of greater importance than the individual merit of the son. In the case of the prodigal son, he was at a greater disadvantage because he was the younger of the two sons and, therefore, less important. Based on the Mosaic law, he was only able to get one third of his father's assets. Moreover, tradition dictated that he did not have much leverage when it came to asking for an unconditional pardon in order that he be restored to his former status. Nobody had to tell him he had brought all of his troubles upon himself.

Among the crowd were Pharisees and teachers of the law (Lk. 15:2). They probably snickered halfway through the story wondering why Jesus was wasting his time talking about a sinner who deserved to be punished severely. There was no need to over analyze this parable. They believed they knew the moral lesson because they were confident they knew the Law. In the mind of the Pharisees, the Law called for death, for this is what was written:

If a man has a stubborn and rebellious son who does not obey his father and mother and will not listen to them when they discipline him, his father and mother shall take hold of him and bring him to the elders at the gate of his town. They shall say to the elders, "This son of ours is stubborn and rebellious. He will not obey us. He is a profligate and a drunkard." Then all the men of his town shall stone him to death (Deut. 21:18-21, NIV).

It was as if this particular law was written having the prodigal son in mind. The description fit him perfectly. He was stubborn and rebellious. We can surmise that he loved to drink, but we are sure that he was a profligate because he recklessly spent every single penny he owned. It was easy for the Pharisees to judge this young man. For them, it would have been better for the prodigal to stay away because his father had the legal right to stone him for his rebellious attitude. They had no idea that Jesus was talking about a different kind of Father.

THE RELIGIOUS SON

While the prodigal son was trying to figure out what he was

going to say to the Father, the eldest son was in the fields working with the servants. His rightful place was in the presence of his father, but he seemed oblivious to the fact that he was a son. He had never understood the heart of the Father, and this severely affected his self-image. The son must connect to the Father, for it is the only way to establish his identity. But, because he spent more time in the fields than in the presence of the father, the eldest son was unable to look intently into the face of his father and discern what was in store for him and the destiny that was before him. Therefore, he behaved like a slave instead of as a son. He manifested the orphan spirit in a different way by acting as if he did not have a home when, in fact, he had legal rights as an heir. Many Christians are just like this eldest son. We are so busy doing good, religious works we fail to take the time to get into the Presence of the Father and look intently into His face to know our place and to find our identity in Him. The orphan spirit often finds its expression in this slave mentality.

The Pharisees and teachers of the law had no idea this particular segment of the story was directly aimed at them. In many respects, they were like the eldest son. They had a privileged position in the Kingdom of God because they were experts of the law. While many, in the ancient world, were groping in spiritual darkness because of ignorance about the power and glory of God, the same thing could not be said of the Pharisees and the teachers of the law. They knew this much: there is only one true God. They also knew that, in the past, this same LORD had manifested His glory in the midst of Israel and, like a mighty eagle, had rescued them from slavery and had brought them to the Land of Promise. They were part of the chosen few; and, according to Paul, these were the people who had been entrusted with the very words of God (Ro. 3:12, NIV). Even though they knew God, they did not seek intimacy but, instead, built a religion around Him.

The same thing can be seen in the Exodus story. The Israelites made clear their intention to simply benefit from their relationship with God but were unwilling to walk with Him as children. They surely wanted God's blessings and what He could do for them, but they did not want anything to do with seeking the Father's face. And so they encouraged Moses to enter into the tent of meeting to commune with the LORD, but the rest of the nation of Israel were content to stay in their tents far away from the Presence of God.

We need to Know and Believe that we have a Father.

Let us "fast forward" to the time when the prodigal son decided to come home and after his father had accepted him as a long lost son and not as a runaway slave. When the eldest son saw the extravagant welcome his father gave his younger son, he was raging mad. He could not understand his father's way of thinking. His father went out to talk to him and pleaded with him to come and celebrate with them. The elder brother refused to come in and retorted:

Look! All these years I've been slaving for you and never disobeyed your orders. Yet you never gave me even a young goat so I could celebrate with my friends. But when this son of yours who has squandered your property with prostitutes comes home, you kill the fattened calf for him! (Lk. 15:29:30, NIV)

Unbeknownst to himself, the orphan spirit was working overtime in the heart of the elder brother; this is why he could not handle the love, compassion, and graciousness of his father. It is something the elder brother was unable to accept because he was a stranger to such things.

A loving person gravitates towards love; a compassionate person gravitates towards mercy; and a gracious person loves nothing more than dispensing grace. In contrast, the person with the orphan heart has only one thing in mind, to create orphans just like himself.

ఞ ఞ

A LOVING PERSON GRAVITATES TOWARDS LOVE.
A COMPASSIONATE PERSON GRAVITATES TOWARDS MERCY, AND A
GRACIOUS PERSON WOULD LOVE NOTHING ELSE THAN TO
DISPENSE GRACE.

ఞ ఞ

The elder brother wanted the younger son to suffer just as he had. The elder son wanted the younger to slave away in the fields and to experience how hard it was to toil under the burning sun. He wanted his brother's hands to be cut and bruised from hard labor, and he wanted his younger brother to work without receiving anything in return. All his life the elder brother had worked like a hired servant on the estate of his father; and, for all those years, he had looked with envy at the resources within his grasp while feeling unable to even glean from the ripened harvest or to feast among his friends with something as insignificant as a roasted young goat. His orphan heart had told him that the truly important stuff was off-limits. The elder brother demanded that everyone adhere to his own standard. His thinking was more like that of the Pharisees and Sadducees in its religious and legalistic striving for acceptance.

The elder brother could not reconcile the idea of a Father giving away gifts for free. The father, on the other hand, was puzzled by the reaction of his eldest son. The father approached him. With just five words the father tried to change and heal the orphan mindset so his son would begin to think like an heir. The father said to him, "Everything I have is yours" (Lk. 15:31, NIV). For as long as the elder brother could remember, he had always been with slaves, so it did not occur to him that he, too, was part of the household and not just a hireling.

~ ~
THE FATHER SAID TO HIM, "EVERYTHING I HAVE IS YOURS."
~ ~

We, too, often have the attitude of a servant, even though we have been fully accepted and welcomed into the Father's house. All He has is ours. We, like the elder son, do not really know the heart of the Father. The elder son must learn to spend more time in the presence of his father.

There is a major difference between knowing there is a Father and believing that He is Father to us. For more than two thousand years, millions of Christian men and women have uttered the Lord's Prayer countless times. Even though they know it by heart, many are unable to enjoy and experience its true potential because this prayer has to be activated correctly. In the opening verse it says, "Our Father in heaven…" Jesus' words demonstrate a correct understanding of who the Father is and where He dwells; but, more importantly, there is the correct emotion that must come to make that utterance potent and effective. No one can say "Father" without affection. In the parable, look at the conversation between the master of the house and his eldest son. Notice that the religious son came grumbling and complaining, but he never once used the title "Father" in his short speech. (Lk. 15:29-30). It is a term of endearment only a true son would know how to use.

We have seen there are actually two brothers in the Parable of the Lost Son. Both of them tried to live life outside the home. The prodigal son decided to put as much distance as he could from his father and spent all his time and money pursuing the things he thought could make him happy and satisfied with life. The devout brother, on the other hand, also lived outside his father's will for he thought he could impress his father by working in the fields along with the slaves. Both of the brothers represent the way the world deals with Father God. Both of them fell short of God's glory and both of them needed to come home.

REFLECTION

Take some time to reflect on the goodness and loving kindness of our Father. He says to you, "Everything I have is yours!"

ACTIVATION

"Search me, O God, and know my heart; test me and know my anxious thoughts. And see if there is any wicked way in me, And lead me in the way everlasting" - Psalm 139:23-24, NIV.

1. Father, show me if there are ways in my life where I choose to act like the rebellious son.

2. Father, show me the areas in my life where I choose to live like the religious son, working as a slave for Your love and inheritance instead of knowing it has all been mine from the very beginning.

DECLARATION

I am not an orphan, I am a son! I am not a slave, I am a son! All that You have is mine. You are my loving Father! There is nothing I can do that can take Your love from me; and there is nothing I can do to make You love me because it is not about the doing. You just love me because I am Yours!

CHAPTER FOUR

THE HOMECOMING

"In love he predestined us to be adopted as his sons through Jesus Christ in accordance with his pleasure and will to the praise of his glorious grace, which he has freely given us in the One he loves."

Ephesians 1:4b-6 (NIV)

A true heir in the Kingdom knows this principle by heart: "In him and through faith in him we may approach God with freedom and confidence" (Eph. 3:12, NIV). A good son will never hesitate to enter in and approach the Father. Children with slave-like tendencies make excuses for why they will not draw near. In the Parable of the Lost Son we can see the root cause of their struggle. Their individual hearts were never intertwined with the Father's. The younger son's distance was a result of willful defiance while the elder brother's refusal to come in was the consequence of a self-righteous attitude, but the time has come for both of them to narrow the gap and enter in.

Throughout the Biblical narrative you will find children with an orphan mindset. They squander opportunities and bring poverty and shame to their families. Interestingly, there is a common link between all of them, which is their inability to draw near to their fathers. They are not willing to stay longer and enjoy the company of their fathers. This orphan mindset can only be reversed by understanding there is a level of intimacy required for father and son to bond.

We can see this principle at work in the household of Abraham. He had two sons. Ishmael was the eldest and Isaac was the younger brother. Although Ishmael was a son, his mother was an Egyptian maidservant who did not live with Abraham. Naturally, the boy was nourished and taken care of in the tent of Hagar, not in main tent where father Abraham lives. The boy grew up with slaves and therefore he had the mentality of an insecure, fearful, needy servant rather than the confidence of a legal heir to one of the richest livestock traders in ancient Palestine. His identity was so fragile that when he saw a feast given to celebrate the birth of Isaac his younger brother, he began to mock the household of his father Abraham (Gen. 21:9). This is why he had to be sent away.

When Isaac was a grown man he married Rebekah and they had two sons, Esau, the firstborn, and Jacob, the younger son. The same pattern of orphan thinking can also be seen in this family because the orphan spirit was with Esau, while the spirit of sonship rested with Jacob. Esau could not wait to get out of the house every morning. He preferred to stay outdoors while Jacob wanted to stay close to his father. Although Isaac loved Esau more than Jacob it was the latter who received the blessing of the father and not the eldest son. This is why Esau lived most of his adult life as a drifter in the desert.

When Jacob was a grown man he also decided to start a family. He had twelve sons in all, but only one behaved like a true son, while the rest set their hearts against their father's will (Gen. 37:23). They were more at home with the animals than with their father. Joseph, on the other hand, knew how to please his father and as a result he received affirmation and splendid gifts such as a multicolored robe. Instead of encouraging his other sons to spend more time with him, Jacob's gift giving drove them to murderous envy and so they sold Joseph to slave traders.

These twelve sons eventually became twelve tribes comprising more than one and a half million people. What was true in the physical was also true in the spiritual. The multitudes had no interest in knowing Father God. During that time, there were only three men who were willing to draw near to the presence of God. Moses, Joshua, and Caleb were ready to pay the price of intimacy. The rest were too timid and lazy to approach Father God. We cannot be of the same spirit. We need to open the door of Father's house, run to him, jump into his lap, and spend a great deal of time in His presence, as He proceeds to teach us and impart upon us, not only the spirit of wisdom, but also the power of His love.

Make no mistake, we are not merely talking about the space between two objects like the expanse that separates a person from religious objects such as a church building or church meetings. It is more about the distance in terms of relationships. For example, Saul lived in Jerusalem and he was near the objects of Jewish religion such as the Temple and the Ark of the Covenant. Compare him to David, who spent a great deal of time in the fields tending his flock. Nevertheless, David was closer to God than Saul. The difference between these two men was the desire of their hearts. This can be seen in the way they spent their time. You can tell the character of the person just by looking how he would use his free time. With regards to David, there is only one thing that could make him truly happy and he revealed it through this psalm:

Better is one day in your courts than a thousand elsewhere; I would rather be a doorkeeper in the house of my God than dwell in the tents of the wicked (Ps. 84:10, NIV).

David was never conflicted when it came to his priorities. He was even willing to be demoted as doorkeeper as long as he was permitted to have a glimpse of Father. But knowing David, he would have just pressed in. He would do everything to be in the court of the King, where only those of royal birth were allowed to come in. This tells us that David was secure in his identity and he would not allow others to deprive him of the opportunity to draw near. If the spirit that flowed through David would have been the same spirit that was with Ishmael then he would not have been content to live in slave's quarters. He would have insisted upon his rights to see the face of his father. If the same spirit was with Esau, he would have never spent his days far away from his father.

HUNGER AND HUMILITY

The prodigal son had to learn the hard way that it is better to dwell in the house of the Father rather than live in the dwelling place of the wicked. He had learned the error of his ways and he was willing to come home and beg his father to hire him as a servant. With just one step, he was homeward bound. However, it took some time for him to reach his country of origin. While he was on the road there was only one thing on his mind, will his father forgive him for the terrible things that he had done? Yet at this point, he was already a broken man and no longer the arrogant and boisterous son he once was. He prepared a statement and he desperately tried to memorize, so as not to stutter when he was face-to-face with his father. So, he kept on rehearsing this speech, "Father, I have sinned against heaven and against you. I am no longer worthy to be called your son; make me like one of your hired men" (Lk. 15:18-19, NIV).

> HE KNEW WHEREVER THE FATHER WENT THERE WOULD BE
> PROVISION AND BLESSING.

In comparison the eldest son's response was rooted in pride. In the words of Jesus, "The older brother became angry and refused to go in" (Lk. 15:28, NIV). He refused to go in. What was the major difference between the two sons? The younger son had learned humility and was hungry for the presence of his father. He did not care if he would be relegated to the position of a slave as long as the father was nearby. He knew wherever the father went there would be provision and blessing. He was hungry for something more than food. He was hungry for the love of his father. While in the pig pen, and under the authority of wicked men, he understood there was nothing in the whole world like the precious love of his father. He spent everything he had in the pursuit of happiness and ended up more miserable than ever.

SELF-SUFFICIENCY AND SELF-RIGHTEOUSNESS

The older brother refused to go in because he thought he deserved to be seated in the seat of honor and clothed with the robe of nobility simply because he was the eldest and more importantly because he worked hard at it.

At this point in the story, as Jesus was telling it to the Pharisees, they were on the edge of their seats. Jesus' words were shooting straight into their hearts like a laser guided missile. The Jewish religion of ancient Israel was so sophisticated it has no equal in terms of complexity and rigidity. There are hundreds of laws and statutes that an orthodox Jew must observe. The average member of the said religion finds it impossible to track every single one of them. And yet the Pharisees memorized every piece of unimportant detail by heart. They were more than fanatical in their approach to serving God. For those who were accepted into this elite circle of religious men, it was hard not be proud. The Father seeks a different kind of worshipper and His requirement for entry is a broken spirit and a contrite heart.

There is another reason why the older brother refused to go in. He never experienced a deep spiritual hunger for his father's provisions. He lived among slaves and worked alongside them and therefore he received the portions designated for slaves. He saw himself as a hired servant and therefore, he behaved as one. At the end of the day he would line up and wait patiently for the daily wages accorded to hirelings. As a consequence he merely had enough. The older brother lived in the periphery of the father's house. He was content to glean from his father's harvest not knowing that all that was contained in the storehouse was his.

The younger son had finally completed the last leg of the journey and was standing in the entrance to the father's estate. Jesus said, "But while he was still a long way off, his father saw him and was filled with compassion for him; he ran to his son, threw his arms around him and kissed him" (Lk. 15:20, NIV). Afterwards, the father passed through the other side of His house to talk with his eldest son who was hurting from self-righteousness. Yes, it is true, spiritual pride comes before a great fall. The father pleaded with him and eventually the two sons were together with him. It was a prophetic picture of the Gentile believers and Jewish believers coming together and living together under one roof and the banner over them is the Father's love.

CROSSING THE GREAT DIVIDE

The Pharisees and the teachers of the law were stunned. They could not believe what they just heard. They thought Jesus had it all mixed up. The younger son was deserving of death. The older brother was supposed to receive the applause of heaven, but the story did not end as they had anticipated. It was a very powerful message which would reverberate through the ages. Jesus made an emphatic statement when taught that parable. It does not matter what you did in the past, it does not even matter what you did yesterday, as long as you are willing to accept you are a prodigal son terribly in need of a home. Once you cross that line, run straight to the Father's welcoming arms and then you will receive the rights and privileges of sonship.

In the same manner, no amount of good deeds can change your status from a slave to a son. The transition will never happen even if you spend your whole life working out there in the fields. The amount of sacrifice you have struggled to put up with over the years pale in comparison to the glory of sonship. This is why this title and privilege cannot be bought by works. It can only be received through faith as we believe in the graciousness and love of the Father.

る る
TRUE SPIRITUAL NOURISHMENT CAN ONLY BE FOUND INSIDE THE FATHER'S HOME.
る る

Let us emulate the example of the repentant son. He had the humility to acknowledge that a good life is only possible when we choose to live under the care, authority and protection of the Father. Aside from that we should develop the same spiritual hunger as exemplified by the younger son. He knew there is real food in the Father's house, for in there he can find the bread of life. On the other hand let us beware the bread of the Pharisees, it can only satisfy in a superficial manner and unable to reach deep down into our being and nourish our impoverished souls. True spiritual nourishment can only be found inside the Father's home. Healing and restoration is also available there. Come let us enter in.

REFLECTION

Father is our home. Picture Him full of love and glory with arms wide open ready to receive you at any time. He is always there waiting for his sons/daughters to run into His arms.

ACTIVATION

1. Father, is there any part of me that is like the prodigal son who has squandered or been careless with my inheritance just to pursue pleasures or desires that will not last?

2. Father, is there any part of me that is like the elder son and where I try to work for what is already mine?

DECLARATION

Father, You are my home! I am confident in who I am and whose I am. I am your son/daughter and I will never hesitate to come into Your presence. I will pursue you like David! Give me a heart after yours. I refuse to live any part of my life in the slave's quarters anymore because I know the palace is my inheritance. I will not live on the outskirts or Your house, but I will boldly and with confidence approach Your throne. I am seated with you in heavenly places. I will live from You, not for You. I will live out of a place of sonship!

CHAPTER FIVE

THE RESTORATION PROCESS

"He will turn the hearts of the fathers to their children, and the hearts of the children to their fathers; or else I will come and strike the land with a curse."
Malachi 4:6 (NIV)

"Yet to all who received him, to those who believed in his name, he gave the right to become children of God."
John 1:12 (NIV)

Stepping into the presence of the Father is just the first step in healing the orphan spirit. We are familiar with stories of cyclical defeats wherein a sinner gets converted only to go back to the pig pen afterwards. The problem is not in the grace of God but in our inability to walk, talk, feel, and think like a true son. For someone who has been an orphan for any length of time a radical transformation has to occur. This change is only possible if we are willing to allow the Spirit of God to restore what was lost in the Garden of Eden, and therefore, allow the Father to rebuild His image and likeness in us so, when He looks into our innerman, He can see the image of Jesus looking back at Him. The orphan spirit cannot be cast out; it can only be displaced by the spirit of sonship through Jesus Christ our Lord.

Let us take a final look at the Parable of the Lost Son. As soon as the prodigal son set foot in his father's house, he was so overjoyed there was nothing else on his mind but the resolve to remain grateful because he had survived a harrowing ordeal. Having vowed never to leave the father's house, he made a strange confession saying, "I am no longer worthy to be called your son" (Lk. 15:21, NIV). Prior to this encounter, he had made an equally strange inner plea when he said, "…make me like one of your hired men" (Lk. 15:19, NIV). If he had been given a chance to utter those terrible words, his fate would have been sealed. He would have become just like the elder brother who wanted the father's blessing but was unable to have any kind of relationship with him. He would have continually struggled to live in his father's house as if he did not belong there.

It is wonderful to know the Father understands what we are thinking. So, before the prodigal son could even say one more word, his father cut him off by saying, "Quick! Bring the best robe and put it on him" (Lk. 15:22, NIV). The prodigal son was thunderstruck by those words. He could not believe what his father said. He knew the significance of the "best robe," and he instantly knew he was going to be restored to his former status.

THE ROBE OF RIGHTEOUSNESS AND IDENTITY

The prodigal son could have protested and groveled like a beggar on his knees. He could have reasoned with his father insisting he was unworthy of such kindness…and he would have been theologically correct. According to the Law, he did not deserve mercy but punishment. Sometimes we try to preach to God and tell Him we know more about Scriptures than He does. When we try to refuse the kindness of God because of our past history and failures, we think we are doing Him a favor. We think He has so many things to do He should not waste His time with a prodigal son.

ôr ৵

THE FATHER FINDS IT HARD TO UNDERSTAND WHY MANY
LEGITIMATE HEIRS BEHAVE LIKE SLAVES.

ôr ৵

If you ever think this way, then welcome to the school of the Pharisees for you will surely graduate with honors! On the contrary, Father God looks at us from a different vantage point. He sees us as sons and daughters. On many occasions, the Father finds it hard to understand why many legitimate heirs behave like slaves, which will be of no benefit to anyone, except perhaps the devil. The whole of creation is pleading with Father to release to them the sons of glory. Yet, those who are already children do not want or do not know how to live in the Father's favor. However, the spirit of sonship will exceedingly and abundantly bless the recipient, no matter how unworthy he thinks he is. Nothing more can give happiness to any father than to see his children walking upright, in authority, and in stewardship of the things he has given them: the same is true of Father God.

There is another reason why the prodigal son did not utter another word after the father ordered him to be clothed. When the father said to get the best robe, the son knew the servant would not run and get it from an ordinary closet. He knew the servant would go straight to the father's closet and bring back a set of clothes the father owned.

‽ ‽

THE BEST WAY TO COVER OUR FEAR AND SHAME IS TO ASK THE FATHER TO CLOTHE US WITH GLORY.

‽ ‽

Like the prodigal, our own clothing is not what the Father wants to see us wearing. You can have the most expensive wardrobe comprised of signature clothing from well known designers, but in the spiritual realm you are still naked. The Father knows this. Heaven is privy to this information. This is why Adam and Eve cried out that they were naked the moment they sinned against God. Just like Adam, we try to remedy the problem by creating our own apparel when the best way to cover our fear and shame is to ask the Father to clothe us with glory.

The insistence to find a solution through our own efforts will not work. There is only one type of clothing that can bring us back to the position we were meant to have. David, after a major setback in his life, did not allow himself to dawdle in the mud because he knew where to turn to for help and he said, "But you are a shield around me, O LORD; you bestow glory on me and lift up my head" (Ps. 3:3, NIV).

Jesus was first stripped naked before he was hung on the cross. He was made naked so He could pass on His clothes to us. When we are restored back to the Father as sons and daughters, we receive the robe of glory Jesus forsook before coming to the earth. This same robe of glory is bestowed upon us to dispel the feeling of helplessness and abandonment.

The robe of righteousness is not only a shield that will silence the accuser of the brethren and quench his fiery darts; it is also a badge of authority because in the spiritual realm it establishes the identity of the owner. The owner of that robe has full access to what the Father owns and no servant of the Father will refuse his request for help.

THE RING OF AUTHORITY

Before they put the prodigal son in the best robe, the servants cleaned him up. When he no longer smelled like pig manure, they clothed him, and everyone stood back to gaze at him in wonder. They finally were able to recognize the former orphan, in tattered clothes, was the father's long lost son. The small crowd that gathered erupted in cheers. However, the father was not yet done with the rebuilding process. He gave a signal to one of the servants to bring in a special box. When it was opened in front of them and the contents were displayed, the son gasped because he saw the signet ring, engraved with the symbol of the family. The ring on his finger represented the power and influence of his father (Ex. 31:18).

IF YOU ARE A SON, THEN YOU ARE EXPECTED TO WORK
ALONGSIDE THE FATHER, BUT NOT AS SLAVES WHO LABOR
WITHOUT HAVING ANY PART OF HIS INHERITANCE.

Through this parable, the Father seems to be saying a son must share the Father's strength, speak on His behalf, and, ultimately, earn the right to inherit everything He owns. The Bible says "the earth is the Lord's and the fullness thereof"; but, the moment Adam was created, he was immediately given a mandate to cultivate the Garden of Eden and to keep it (Gen. 2:15). The garden was owned by God; however, He gave it to His son. This was no ordinary piece of land. There were four riverheads with their own storehouses of precious resources. One riverhead alone, the Pishon has gold, precious minerals, and aromatic resin, which is a raw material for perfume (Gen. 2:11). Just as Adam was to steward the land God had given him, if you are a son, then you are expected to work alongside the Father, but not as slaves who labor without having any part in His inheritance. He has given you the position as a son and we need to move in His authority. Accept the signet ring because you will need it to do mighty works for your Father.

RESTORING THE WHOLE PERSON

The next thing the father did was to give the prodigal son a pair of sandals to clothe his feet. This may seem trivial for many of us and, ironically, this is the reason why Jesus highlighted this step in the restoration process. We always consider our feet as the least important part of our body. We spend a great deal of money to pamper and take care of our face, hands, and body, but not usually the feet. This was especially true in ancient times. This is why Jesus washed His disciples' feet to show them how much He cared for them.

Jesus' actions spoke louder than words. He demonstrated what the Father thinks of us and now we know the Lord is willing to go to the lowest point of our being, the dirtiest and the smelliest, and will heal that festering wound so we can stand upright as a true son, able to walk in His ways.

The kiss to the face, the best robe, the signet ring, and the sandals on the feet ministered to the mind, body, soul, and spirit of the prodigal son. The restoration process had to be holistic. It had to cover everything: and, by doing so, the prodigal son received complete healing of his mind and emotions. The orphan spirit was pulled out from the roots, never to grow back again.

The rebuilding process was so thorough the father even went as far as sealing the new relationship with a covenant. He commanded the fattened calf to be slaughtered. The blood of the covenant sealed the promise in which the son had a permanent place in the house of the father, and there was nothing he could do to change his father's love for him or to alter his position as a son in the father's house. His father finalized the restoration process with a joyous celebration signaling everyone to honor His son just as they would honor him.

RESTORING THE RELIGIOUS

After restoring his wayward child, the father focused his attention on his eldest son. However, this son might have been a tougher challenge than the first. Jesus said he did not come for the righteous but for sinners (Mk. 2:17). As long as the elder brother continued to believe he could work his way into the heart of his father, he could never experience true sonship and would never receive what was graciously given to his prodigal brother.

We don't know what really happened to the elder brother. Jesus sort of created a "cliffhanger," presumably for the benefit of the Pharisees and the experts of the Law who were in attendance. Jesus knew they understood the ramifications of the story and, therefore, had to make a decision afterwards. Nevertheless, if we really want to know what happened to the elder brother in the parable, then we can read other examples in the Bible. We will discover there were two Pharisees who spent a lifetime working outside the Father's embrace, but, after a personal encounter with Jesus, had a change of heart and accepted the invitation of the Father to come home. The first one was Nicodemus and the second one was Saul of Tarsus.

The testimonies of Nicodemus and Saul of Tarsus tell us how committed the Father is when it comes to rescuing those who are blinded by self-righteousness and religion. The Father did not rest until He was able to convince the elder brother to carry the yoke of sonship and not that of slavery. Moreover, the experience of Nicodemus and Saul, in the presence of God, will reveal to us what a complete restoration process can do to a person ready to let go of striving and self-aggrandizement.

The first Pharisee to come home was Nicodemus. He was no ordinary Pharisee. He was a member of the Jewish ruling council (Jn. 3:1). This made him not only an expert of the Law but also a devout follower of the Jewish religion. He had dedicated his life to being a slave to regulations, and yet he knew there was something missing in his life.

He went to Jesus at night so that his colleagues would not see him talking to the Lord. (Jn. 3:2). It was not very courageous of him, but Jesus did not mind. He understood the struggle inside of Nicodemus. We don't need to be perfect when we come to the Lord; just a small step in the right direction is all the Father needs. In response, Jesus gave him the gift of everlasting life. It was to Nicodemus that the famous John 3:16 verse was first given: "For God so loved the world that he gave his one and only Son, that whoever believes in him shall not perish but have eternal life" (NIV). For Nicodemus, the restoration process was not just a simple makeover; he experienced a rebirth (Jn. 3:7).

The story of Saul of Tarsus, on the other hand, will give flesh to the born again experience. Here is a man who was totally deceived by his fanaticism to Judaism. He was willing to kill Christians and drag them to jail to prove his devotion. Deep down in his heart he really wanted to know more about the one true God. He was a murderer, arrogant, and self-assured; yet, even these glaring flaws did not prevent Jesus from accepting Saul into His Kingdom.

Saul of Tarsus had the orphan spirit; and, for it to be dislodged, he had to go through a process. First, he fell off his high horse, which symbolized his religious pride. Second, he was blinded by the glory of God, reminding him that he did not have what it takes to see God. His righteousness was like a filthy rag in the presence of the Lord. Finally, when he acknowledged the pruning and the healing touch of the Father, he experienced a name change to complete the restoration process of Paul the Apostle.

We have seen two groups of people living outside Father's love. Both had the orphan spirit rooted within their very core. Yet, the Father did not have a hard time displacing this foul spirit with the Spirit of His Son Jesus. The only thing required is humility and the longing to enter into His rest. We don't even have to figure everything out in order for Father to accept us and experience the wonderful blessing of sonship. We just have to take one step and the Father will run to us, lift our head, clothe us with the best robe, place the ring of authority on our finger, heal our crippled walk, and seal it all with a covenant, pledging we will always be a son and nothing can separate us from the Father.

REFLECTION

The mercy and love of the Father is amazing. He took extraordinary lengths to restore back to us our identity, our inheritance, and our position as sons/daughters. Reflect on those actions.

ACTIVATION

1. Father, you have clothed me in your righteousness. Please show me if I am still wearing anything you did not clothe me with.

2. Father, I can not afford to see or think about myself any differently than you do. So, show me any lie I believe about myself. I only want to see myself and others the way you do.

DECLARATION

Father, you have restored all things. I am your son/daughter! My identity and position are solely found in you. You have clothed me in your righteousness and glory! As a son/daughter you have entrusted me with authority and I will co-labor with you to restore all things and steward what you have given to me.

CHAPTER SIX

FATHER'S AMAZING LOVE

"How great is the love the Father has lavished on us, that we should be called children of God! And that is what we are! The reason the world does not know us is that it did not know him. Dear friends, now we are children of God, and what we will be has not yet been made known. But we know that when he appears we shall be like him, for we shall see him as he is."

1 John 3:1-2 (NIV)

When we witness something amazing, we usually applaud, express unbelief, or sometimes draw back in fear. Anger, however, is not normally an emotion associated with an unexpected event. Yet, when the Pharisees saw something too wonderful to understand, they became indignant. Their anger was aimed at Jesus and His friends. They could not believe that Jesus, a supposedly righteous teacher, was actually having fun! He ate and talked with sinners, rubbed elbows with greedy tax agents, received food prepared by prostitutes, and answered questions asked by petty thieves and crooks.

Everyone was smiling and enjoying the teachings and encouragement of Jesus Christ—except for the religious men from Jerusalem. The Pharisees were red-hot angry like a volcano about to erupt. They could not allow this abomination to continue. In their estimation, these sinners did not qualify to receive favor. They failed the test and missed the mark, so they must be forbidden to partake of the

Lord's Table. Jesus, sensing the Pharisees' religious fervor, stood up and told the story of a father and his two sons.

Jesus did not begin his story with words like "rebellion," "perversion," or "prodigal." He simply said there was a father who had two sons. At the end of the story, Jesus focused on a loving Father, not on the sins of the children. Bible scholars and a great number of commentators have missed this very crucial fact because religion distorts our worldview. Religion focuses on the sin and the sinner but never on the gracious Father, who loves nothing more than to be with His children. He desires to be in close proximity regardless whether or not they are worthy of His presence. Thus, I believe this parable should have been entitled *The Parable of the Loving Father.*

RELIGION'S DEATHTRAP

I can still remember what it felt like to be under the influence of drugs and the devil. It was not a great feeling. I staggered like a drunkard in a dark world without the presence of God guiding me. Fear and shame were my constant companions and offered me no real comfort, only pain. I longed to be in the security and comfort of home. Like the prodigal son, I was glad to be given a second chance. I went home to the open arms of both the Father and my earthly family. It should have been a happy ending, but then I went to church and began to follow rules instead of cultivating a healthy relationship with the Father.

I went from being a prodigal son to being the elder brother. I tried to win the favor of the Father by working tirelessly. Every waking moment was given to the altar of religion. After a few months of being in church, I got the hang of man-made rules and became adept at being a slave in my Father's house. What irony! After a while, I became a taskmaster myself, a religious person making life miserable for those who were already in church and making it difficult for outsiders to enter in. I remember what Jesus said to the religious leaders of His day:

"Woe to you, teachers of the law and Pharisees, you hypocrites! You shut the kingdom of heaven in men's faces. You yourselves do not enter, nor will you let those enter who are trying to" (Mt. 23:13, NIV).

I was guilty of the same thing. Many churchgoers are also guilty of the trap of religion. We come in, assess a situation, and make up our minds about people who are not supposed to be in church. This creates a test which is impossible for people to pass because it requires a perfect score before they are allowed to enter the presence of God.

Jesus attempted to break through the Pharisees' shallow thinking. Jesus wanted them to focus on the most important thing, which is the love of the Father. The religious leaders were focused on the Law, but Jesus wanted them to see the Giver of the law. They were awed by the Creator and His creations, but Jesus wanted to usher them into the presence of the Father.

Jesus knew his Father. Every time Jesus was challenged to prove His identity, He would always point to the Father. His identity was closely intertwined with that of His Father. Whenever the Pharisees tried to discredit Him, Jesus would tell them He knew the Father and the Father knew Him. Jesus wanted everyone to be like Himself—to eat, breathe, and sleep spiritual intimacy with the Father in heaven.

THE FATHER'S EMBRACE

The passion of Jesus to reveal the core nature of the Father is fueled by the joy and exhilaration of knowing Him. Jesus could not keep silent regarding the manner in which the Pharisees treated people. He had to rebuke them because He saw how far they were from the truth. Father is the God of Love, full of grace and compassion for a lost and dying world. It would be a tremendous injustice for men and women, created in the image and likeness of God, not to have a correct view of the Father. Jesus came to set the record straight.

ॐ ॐ
JESUS DID NOT TALK ABOUT THE LOVE OF GOD BASED ON WHAT
HE KNEW FROM READING SCRIPTURES.
ॐ ॐ

Jesus did not talk about the love of God based on what He knew from reading Scriptures. Although a person with great insight and deep longing to understand the words of God can receive the same revelation of the goodness of the Father, Jesus' revelation did not simply come from studying the words of God but from an intense personal experience.

Jesus grew up with the Spirit of His Father by His side. He was full of the Holy Spirit and was led by the Spirit (Lk. 4:1). Jesus had the most intimate walk with Father, carried His Father's presence with Him at all times, and was able to hear the Father's voice directing Him in the way He should go. Not only did Jesus carry the presence of His Father wherever He went, but He could also access the heart and mind of Father, and, therefore, could be led by the Spirit of God.

Jesus knew the love and goodness of Father. Nobody had to tell Him second-hand stories about Father's love. He knew the details intimately. There was a real connection between Father and Son. It was a give-and-take relationship where the Father poured out His great love while the Son received everything with joy and thanksgiving. A glimpse of that special relationship was given for our benefit. Let us go to the baptism of Jesus in the River Jordan and enjoy a frontseat view of the event:

As soon as Jesus was baptized, he went up out of the water. At that moment heaven was opened, and he saw the Spirit of God descending like a dove and lighting on him. And a voice from heaven said, "This is my Son, whom I love; with him I am well pleased (Mt. 3:16-17).

ॐ ॐ

JESUS KNEW THE LOVE AND GOODNESS OF FATHER. NOBODY HAD TO TELL HIM SECOND-HAND STORIES ABOUT FATHER'S LOVE; HE KNEW THE DETAILS INTIMATELY.

ॐ ॐ

Jesus saw with His own eyes heaven being ripped open so the Spirit of the Father could be released and joined with His Son. He saw the Spirit of His Father descend gently as a dove. He had the assurance the Father would be with Him every minute of every single day. If that were not enough, the Father spoke to those who had discernment and said the following words: "This is my Son, whom I love; with him I am well pleased." Jesus not only saw and heard this, but He also had the witness of John the Baptist who could validate what He knew. Thus, Jesus was assured of the truth of the Father's love.

ॐ ॐ

THIS RELATIONSHIP HE HAD WITH HIS FATHER TRANSFORMED
THE WAY HE SAW THE WORLD AND RADICALLY ALTERED HIS
ATTITUDE AND WAY OF LIFE.

ॐ ॐ

This relationship Jesus had with His Father transformed the way He saw the world and radically altered His attitude and way of life. Because of His amazing relationship with the Father, Jesus became mighty in word and deed. He turned the world upside down and then right side up once again.

ॐ ॐ

THE FATHER'S EMBRACE BECAME HIS SOURCE OF STRENGTH
AND POWER.

ॐ ॐ

The Father's embrace became Jesus' source of strength and power which enabled Him to say great things. He said He could help us overcome the devil and the world. He said He can give us life to the fullest. He said those who are weary must stop struggling and give their heavy burden to Him. The love of the Father was so real, intense, and powerful that Jesus was able to do the extraordinary and the impossible. Jesus revealed to us this special relationship does not end between Father and Son. This love is so real. They want to share it with others.

ॐ ॐ

THE LOVE OF THE FATHER WAS SO REAL, INTENSE, AND POWER-
FUL THAT JESUS WAS ABLE TO DO THE EXTRAORDINARY AND THE
IMPOSSIBLE.

ॐ ॐ

THE SACRIFICE OF THE FATHER

The loving Father embracing His son Jesus has brought tremendous blessing to the world. This love cannot be contained within the Trinity itself, for it is the nature of the Father to pour out that love. The love that exists within the core of the Triune Godhead is love in the highest and purest form. This kind of love is so amazing it is willing to sacrifice comfort, happiness, and security for the sake of the beloved. The object of the Father's affection is man, and, therefore, the Father has decided He will do everything in His power to save mankind from the everlasting consequence of sin. The love of the Father was made manifest when He gave His only Son.

We have to understand how much it pained the Father to offer His one and only Son on the altar of sacrifice. He had nothing more precious than His Son, for Jesus came from the Father's bosom, so a part of Him would die if He allowed His Son to be used a ransom to cancel the effect of sin. By doing so, the Father demonstrated His commitment to all of us.

OUR RESPONSE

The love of the Father and the sacrifice He made is the ultimate antidote to the orphan spirit. It can only be received, not achieved. We need to learn how to receive it and then live worthy of such a gift.

In *The Parable of the Loving Father* there is a fact we usually ignore. It is the presence of a third son, the faithful and good child, the Son of God. He alone was able to model what it meant to have a true spirit of sonship. Jesus' obedience and submission to the Father was painfully illustrated in the bittersweet declaration, "For God so loved the world that He gave His one and only Son that whoever believes in Him shall not perish but have eternal life." (Jn. 3:16, NIV). We rejoice upon hearing this wonderful news but immediately recoil in horror when we fully understand that, in order for this love to be manifested, the Father had to turn His face away and abandon His child while the Son of God hung on a cross, suffering from the onslaught of sin.

Jesus knew what it was going to take for us to have eternal life; yet, He never once showed fear or hesitation. He was willing to drink the cup of suffering to please His Father. More importantly, Jesus was of one mind with the Father concerning Their goal of redeeming the world. In fact, Jesus revealed to His disciples that He is actually the "firstborn among many." He had to die so the Father could give others the right to become His children as evidenced in this scripture:

For those God foreknew he also predestined to be conformed to the likeness of his Son, that he might be the firstborn among many brothers. And those he predestined, he also called; those he called, he also justified; those he justified, he also glorified (Rom. 8:29-30, NIV).

The Father is longing to have the same kind of relationship with us as He had with Jesus. The only thing we need to do is to receive by faith the love of Father. With this level of supernatural disclosure regarding the great and awesome love of the Father, we are compelled to respond with the same passion and dedication. By doing so, we will not only be healed of the orphan spirit, we will also be conformed into the likeness of His Son; and, therefore, we will be justified and then glorified.

REFLECTION

How great is the love our Father has lavished on us. Take time to reflect on the magnitude of His love and thank Him for His loving pursuit of us.

ACTIVATION

1. Father, I'm not sure I know how to be a son/daughter like Jesus was...full of love, full of the spirit, only doing what the Father does. Jesus, you were the perfect example of how to be a son completely connected to his father, so show me how.

2. Father, show me any religious paradigms or requirements I have made for myself or others you do not have. I don't want to maintain any barriers which would hinder me or others to fully embrace intimacy with you.

DECLARATION

Father, only your love can cast away an orphan spirit. I receive the fullness of your love! My identity is found in you. I want to be full of the spirit and completely led by the spirit. Your love and embrace are my source of strength and power!. I desire to have the same relationship with you that Jesus did. Holy Spirit, help me walk in an intimate love relationship with my Father!

CHAPTER SEVEN

Bringing Many Sons to Glory

"For it was fitting for Him, for whom are all things, and through whom are all things, in bringing many sons to glory, to perfect the author of their salvation through sufferings."

Hebrews 2:10 (NASB)

"The Spirit Himself bears witness with our spirit that we are children of God, and if children, then heirs—heirs of God and joint heirs with Christ, if indeed we suffer with Him, that we may also be glorified together"

Romans 8:16-17 (NKJV)

The love of the Father is too wonderful to comprehend. We are blessed beyond measure simply knowing that He is patient with us and is longing for the day we will learn to walk as true sons and daughters of God. He is also patient in drawing us near and, for those who choose to develop a personal relationship, Father becomes the faithful Author and Finisher of their faith. The Bible is also very clear that those who place their trust in Jesus will not only be saved but will also become a member of God's family.

ॐ ॐ

FATHER HAS ENTRUSTED TO US THIS GOOD NEWS
OF THE KINGDOM

ॐ ॐ

We become part of that heavenly family through unconditional love and amazing grace. We receive this gift through faith and not through works. Nevertheless, membership in this family also requires we work as one family. Father has entrusted to us this good news of the Kingdom. He is asking us to bring many sons to glory as this is Father's greatest desire. Satan's chief joy is to separate children from God, while the Father's delight is to turn their hearts back to Him.

The Parable of the Lost Son can be considered a jewel in a set of parables Luke grouped together in one section of his gospel. Beginning in the fourteenth chapter and ending in the fifteenth, Luke focused on five parables with a similar theme. The others are the *Parable of the Great Banquet, Parable of the Lost Sheep, Parable of the Lost Coin, and finally the Parable of the Lost Son.* We can see why Luke bundled these five parables together. It is clear from reading each one that these stories talk about a God who longs to be reconnected with His children because they are more precious than everything He owns; and, when they return to Him, He will mark that special occasion with a joyous banquet.

It is easy to see the common thread that connects these five parables; it is none other than the love of the Father, which compels Him to run after His erring children. He runs after them like a shepherd who is unable to sleep knowing one of His precious lambs is not yet in the sheep pen. He searches for them like a desperate woman who lost her precious coin and will not rest until she has found it. He waits for them like a father whose son left home and vowed never to return. The Father waits, searches, and runs after those who do not deserve His love, and yet He gives it anyway. And now He turns to us, His spiritual sons and daughters, asking us to partner with Him in His desire to bring many children to His glory.

THE FATHER'S JOY

Jesus was sent to our world to convey a message from the heart of Father God. Jesus made this known to us when He said, "For the Son of Man came to seek and to save that which was lost." Jesus did not just speak these words. His three and a half years of ministry backed up the Father's message.

ð ∾

BOTH THE RELIGIOUS AND THE REBELLIOUS HAVE NO HOPE
APART FROM KNOWING GOD AS THEIR FATHER.

ð ∾

Our theology, no matter how complex and grand, means nothing if we will not follow the example of Christ. His mission was the Father's mission, to seek and save the lost and bring them back to the Father's house. The end goal of everything we do, while we are still here on earth, is to reach out to those who are about to perish for lack of knowledge and are ignorant about the most important truth: there is a loving Father waiting for them. Both the religious and the rebellious have no hope apart from knowing God as their Father.

ð ∾

A SON WHO IS DEVOTED TO HIS FATHER WILL DO EVERYTHING
HIS FATHER SAYS.

ð ∾

Jesus was able to do everything needed to save a sick and dying world because He fully submitted himself to the Father. When Jesus came to earth, He did not come as Lord; He came as an obedient Son of God. A son who is devoted to his father will do everything his father says. More importantly, a son knows what can make his father extremely happy, and he will do everything in his power to bring joy to his father's heart.

THE FUTURE FAMILY OF GOD

For many believers, evangelism and missions has become so institutionalized it is no longer a labor of love but has now become an obligation. Pastors and missions directors constantly talk about the need to evangelize the community and create committees to improve the missions involvement of the local church. Yet, after a few months these initiatives begin to fizzle. This is because many are unable to see the community and the mission field from the Father's point of view.

While we see demographics like the necessity of church growth and the obligation to go to the ends of the earth, the Father is thinking about His future family. It has always been His goal since the beginning of time to build a family, a kingdom of priests, the ecclesia, His sons and daughters through adoption in Jesus Christ.

IN THE KINGDOM OF HEAVEN THE MOST IMPORTANT FEATURE…
IS THE FAMILY OF GOD.

It is God's will to rule the earth through a holy family. In the Kingdom of Heaven, the most important feature is not the gemstones, the streets of gold, the pearly gates, or the other wonderful things one can see there – it is the family of God which is the centerpiece. When the Apostle John described the Kingdom, we are given an idea as to what is keeping it all together as he wrote:

The twelve gates were twelve pearls, each gate made of a

single pearl. The great street of the city was of pure gold, like transparent glass. I did not see a temple in the city, because the Lord God Almighty and the Lamb are its temple. The city does not need the sun or the moon to shine on it, for the glory of God gives it light, and the Lamb is its lamp (Rev. 21:21-23, NIV).

John was a faithful Jew, and so, when he was given a chance to see the city of God, the first thing he did was to locate the temple. Even though John knew where to look because the temple was usually in the center of the city, John could not find this very important structure; instead, he saw the Lord God Almighty who is the Father, and the Lamb who is His Son Jesus taking the place of the temple. Their loving relationship is the power source which lights up heaven and sustains it. Their loving relationship is the model for building God's future family. John the Beloved painted a beautiful illustration of that intimate relationship: Jesus is the lamp and the Father is the light of the lamp!

We are certain a vital part of the Father's plan is to have a family because He revealed it to us in the Book of Genesis. He created Adam in His image and likeness, creating a mini-replica of Himself. If that is not reproduction, then what is? Afterwards He created Eve, and then man and woman were commanded to multiply. What is the purpose of multiplication if not to create a family? But there is more. The Father does not simply desire a family; He wants His children to walk and talk just like Him. In order to clarify what He meant He sent Jesus to model the kind of behavior and mindset He longs to reproduce in us. (Gal. 4:19).

HEIRS AND CO-LABORERS

Jesus is our model. He is our pattern for living. Our identity is secure in Him, and we have the right to be children of God because of what He has done. There is more: whatever inheritance Jesus will receive, we also become co-heirs and receive. However, the Apostle Paul was quick to point out the condition for co-inheritors and this is what he said:

The Spirit himself testifies with our spirit that we are God's children. Now if we are children, then we are heirs—heirs of God and co-heirs with Christ, if indeed we share in his sufferings in order that we may also share in his glory (Romans 8:16-17).

Let us be clear…we can only be saved through faith and not through works so that no one can boast (Eph. 2:8). However, Paul was not talking about salvation; he was talking about future glory. We share not only in the inheritance of the Son of God but also in His glory if we are also able to share in His sufferings.

What kind of suffering was Paul trying to communicate here? We can get an idea by taking a step backwards and trying to comprehend the Epistle to the Romans. What was Paul's main goal in writing this letter? We read in the opening remarks where Paul gave the framework for his ministry stating he had received grace and apostleship "…to call people from among all the Gentiles to the obedience that comes from faith" (Rom. 1:5, NIV). We can, therefore, conjecture that the "suffering" he mentioned is linked to the trials and testing he encountered when he tried to preach the gospel to Jews first and then to the Gentiles.

Although Paul was reluctant to talk about his sufferings in Christ because he thought it was akin to boasting in the flesh, he, nevertheless, provided a glimpse into the kind of distress he went through for the sake of the gospel by declaring:

I have worked much harder, been in prison more frequently, been flogged more severely, and been exposed to death again and again. Five times I received from the Jews the forty lashes minus one. Three times I was beaten with rods, once I was stoned, three times I was shipwrecked, I spent a night and a day in the open sea, I have been constantly on the move. I have been in danger from rivers, in danger from bandits, in danger from my own countrymen, in danger from Gentiles; in danger in the city, in danger in the country, in danger at sea; and in danger from false brothers. I have labored and toiled and have often gone without sleep; I have known hunger and thirst and have often gone without food; I have been cold and naked (2Cor. 11:23-27, NIV).*

All these he endured because of the exceeding glory he would inherit through Christ Jesus. Paul, however, was motivated far beyond any prize promised to him. He only mentioned in passing about the future glory prepared for the co-inheritors of the Son of God, yet he spent a great deal of time discussing the real motivation for ministry and why he continued to preach to the Jews and to the Gentiles. This is what was burning in his heart:

How, then, can they call on the one they have not believed in? And how can they believe in the one of whom they have not heard? And how can they hear without someone preaching to them? And how can they preach unless they are sent? As it is written, "How beautiful are the feet of those who bring good news! (Rom. 10:14-15, NIV).

ೞ ໑

THE FAMILY THE FATHER STARTED…WILL EVENTUALLY BECOME A KINGDOM FILLED WITH SONS AND DAUGHTERS OF GOD WHO ARE KNOWN BY THE LOVE THEY HAVE FOR ONE ANOTHER.

ೞ ໑

If we are children then we are co-heirs. If we are co-heirs, then we are definitely part of the family of God. Furthermore, if we are family, then we are all in this together. The family of God is in the business of multiplication and nurturing so when the end is near, the family the Father started in Garden of Eden will eventually become a Kingdom filled with sons and daughters of God who are known by the love they have for one another.

BRINGING MANY SONS TO GLORY

We can only multiply if we have the Spirit of Jesus within us. This was the distinguishing mark of all the saints belonging to the first century A.D. (Ac. 16:7). Since they had Jesus within them, they worked like the Lord did when he was still here on earth. Jesus set forth the principle when He proclaimed, "I tell you the truth, the Son can do nothing by himself; he can do only what he sees his Father doing, because whatever the Father does the Son also does. For the Father loves the Son and shows him all he does." (Jn. 5:19-20, NIV).

What exactly did Jesus do? Aside from healing the sick, performing miracles, and setting free the spiritually oppressed, Jesus preached the good news and He called out and taught His disciples. He chose twelve men to be His constant companions while teaching them the ways of the Father. From among this number, three were chosen to become the future leaders of the Church He would eventually establish first in Jerusalem, Judea, and Samaria, and then to the ends of the earth. If we desire to know more statistics, Jesus had a solid team of at least 120 disciples who remained with Him even after He was captured, crucified, and considered dead (Ac. 1:15). This group served as the catalyst which catapulted the message of Jesus throughout Palestine, along the Mediterranean, to Rome, and then to the ends of the earth.

Jesus was just like the Father. He was patient in seeking out the lost, and having found them, He took care of them, releasing them from oppression, binding up their wounds, and leading them home to the Father. His commission before He ascended to heaven is clearly shown in the following statement:

All authority in heaven and on earth has been given to me. Therefore go and make disciples of all nations, baptizing them in the name of the Father and of the Son and of the Holy Spirit, and teaching them to obey everything I have commanded you. And surely I am with you always, to the very end of the age (Mt. 28-19-20, NIV).

Jesus initiated the process by instructing us to make disciples of all nations and sealing them with a holy baptism in the name of the holy family: the Father, Son, and Holy Spirit. The Apostle Paul, on the other hand, was allowed to see the end result of discipleship in "…bringing many sons to glory. (Heb. 2:10). Paul used four crucial terms here; let us take a closer look. He said: 1) bring; 2) many; 3) sons; and 4) glory. These four must work together. These terms must be present in our evangelistic activities and in our missionary endeavors. We must bring many sons to the Father so that they will share in His glory.

We must bring them and, therefore, this requires our active participation. We must bring many, and this means we cannot be selective. We must go into the mega-cities and the suburbs, the rural areas as well as the isolated islands. In the *Parable of the Great Banquet*, we are told that the Father is preparing a great feast and, therefore, we are instructed to "Go out to the roads and country lanes and make them come in, so that my house will be full" (Lk. 14:23, NIV). It has to be many; it has to be for glory; and they must all be sons and daughters. Finally we have to co-labor and bring them in. Let us make haste; the Father is waiting.

REFLECTION

Take time to reflect on the Father's heart for his lost sons and daughters.

ACTIVATION

1. Jesus was on the Father's mission to bring sons and daughters back home to the Father. How can I be more about my Father's business?

2. Father, show me anything in my life which would get in the way of leading your sons and daughters home.

DECLARATION

Father, thank you for your relentless pursuit of bringing your sons and daughters back to glory. I want to always be about my Father's business! From the beginning you had a plan for a family and I will help bring sons and daughters back to your house where they belong! I want to see your house full!

GLOBAL MISSION AWARENESS

To find more information about upcoming events,
conferences, international ministry trips
or to purchase items from our
webstore please visit out website at:

www.globalmissionawareness.com

BAPTISM OF LOVE

CD - $7.00

Most Christians can say they have been baptized in water, but have you received God's baptism of love? In this teaching, Leif talks about the drastic change in his life when he received this baptism. Without the baptism of love from our Heavenly Father how can we impart His love to others

HEALING THE ORPHAN SPIRIT

Father God never intended to have a bunch of orphans try to live for God but sons and daughters living from God. The biggest crisis in our families is children living as orphans. The Bible is the story of a loving Father waiting for sons and daughters to come home. There is no place like home. There is an inheritance waiting for you. Come join the family party!

CD - $7.00
DVD - $15.00

ROOTED AND GROUNDED IN LOVE

CD - $7.00

We all desire to be firmly rooted and grounded in God's perfect love. Learn through this Kingdom Revelation message that this only comes when you know "Whose You Are" and "Who You Are!"

CD - $7.00
DVD $15.00

DARE TO DREAM

It is time to revive those dreams and Dare To Dream with Papa God! Romans 8 tells us "the earth is groaning for the sons of God to be revealed." Why? Because Papa wants us to dream with Him, release the kingdom, and see a world changed for His glory. What the world needs is inside of you! So be daring and dream unreasonably with your Papa God!

FATHER LOVES YOU SERIES

This set of 5 sermons on the Love of the Father will draw you into a closer relationship with Father God and reveal to you the heart of God.

CD set - $30.00

CD - $7.00
DVD - $15.00

SPIRIT OF SONSHIP

Elijah raised up a son, Elisha, to carry out his assignment after he was taken to heaven in a whirlwind. Elisha received an inheritance (double portion) from Elijah, his father. Slaves and servants receive pay...sons and daughters receive inheritance.

GMA
INTERNATIONAL
MINISTRY TRIPS

GMA Ministry Trips are the experience of a lifetime.

The purpose of our International Ministry Trips is to
proclaim the salvation of the Kingdom,
the love of the Father,
and demonstrate signs, wonders, and miracles
to those desperately in need of our message.

Are you ready for a Kingdom adventure?

go to

www.globalmissionawareness.com/events